BUILD YOUR OWN ADVENTURE

Contents

Meet Liza

Liza is an adventurous girl who lives in Heartlake City. She has lots of friends there—you'll meet some of them in this book! Liza is a keen gardener and loves being outdoors. She enjoys exploring the sights of her home city, and discovering new places and people.

Family

Liza's cousin, Mia, is also one of her closest friends. Liza looks up to Mia, who is one year older than her. They share a love of the outdoors.

Liza's favorite striped jersey

Cool summer shorts

Comfortable sandals

Liza's Touring Car

Liza has a new touring car. It's a convertible, so she can feel the breeze in her hair and smell the sweet summer flowers. Turn the page to find instructions on how to build this model. Build it and take Liza on some new adventures!

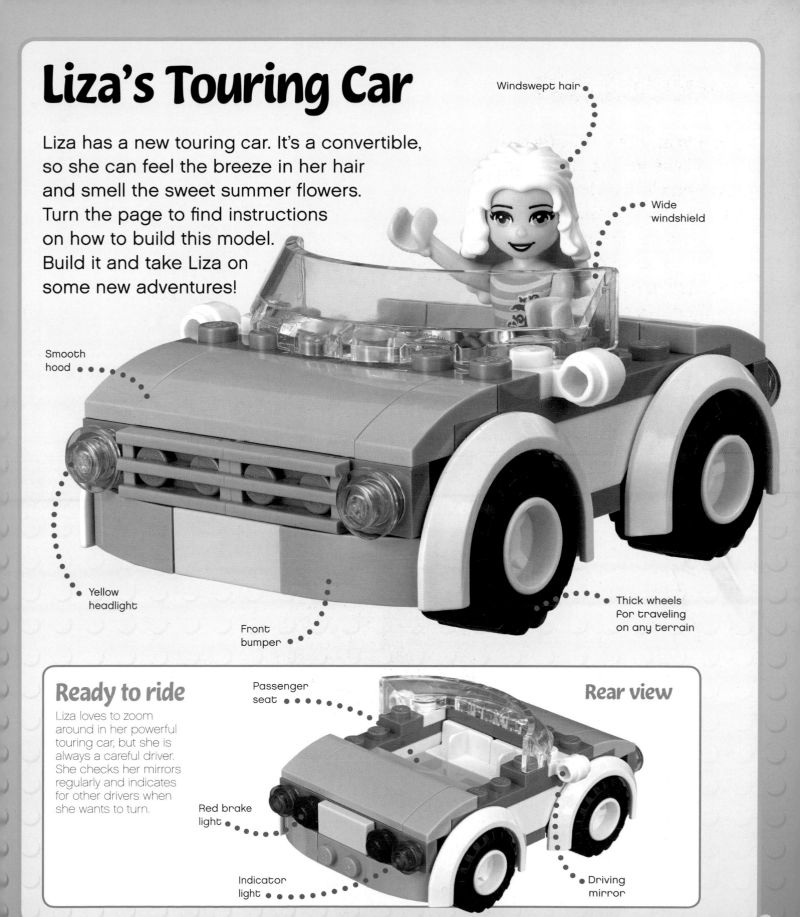

Windswept hair

Wide windshield

Smooth hood

Yellow headlight

Front bumper

Thick wheels for traveling on any terrain

Ready to ride

Liza loves to zoom around in her powerful touring car, but she is always a careful driver. She checks her mirrors regularly and indicates for other drivers when she wants to turn.

Passenger seat

Rear view

Red brake light

Indicator light

Driving mirror

Touring Car instructions

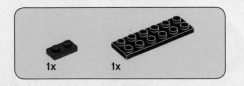

1x   1x

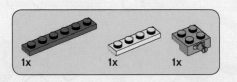

1x   1x   1x

1

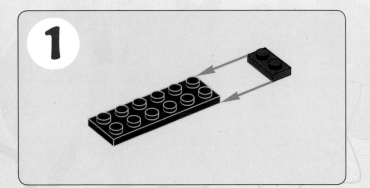

3

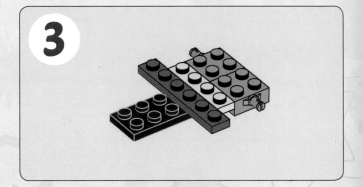

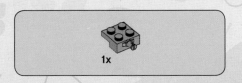

1x

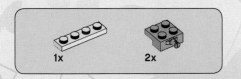

1x   2x

2

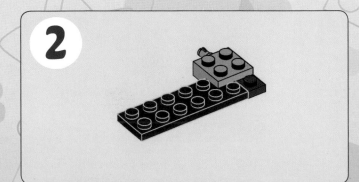

4

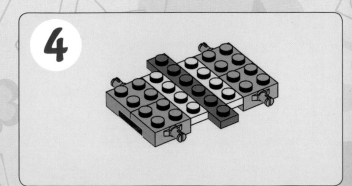

1x

5

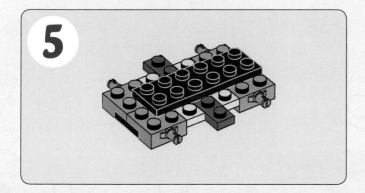

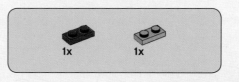

1x 1x

7

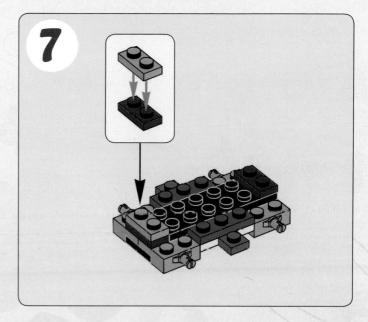

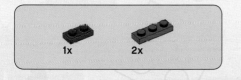

1x 2x

6

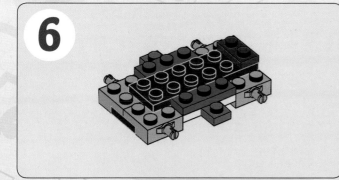

2x

8

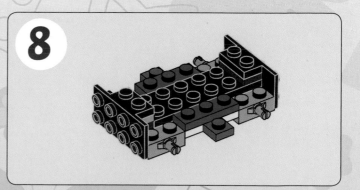

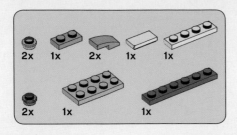

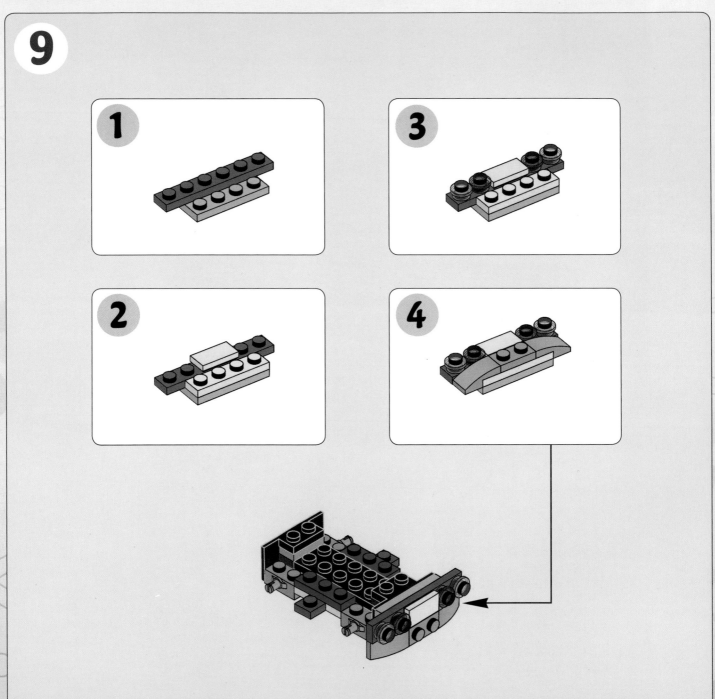

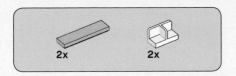

2x   2x

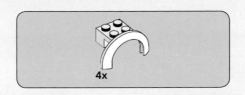

4x

10

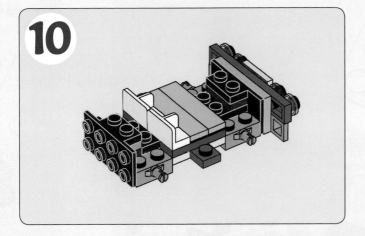

12

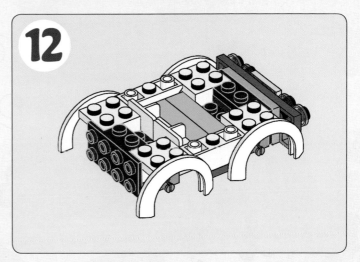

My touring car is starting to take shape.

2x

11

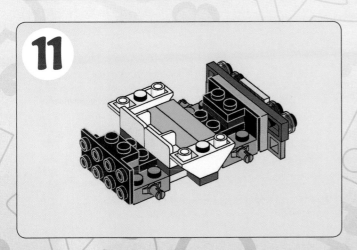

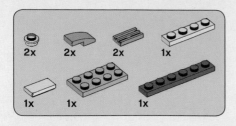

2x 2x 2x 1x

1x 1x 1x

13

1

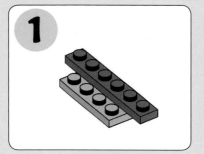

2

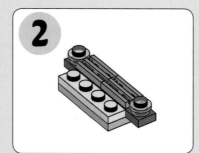

3

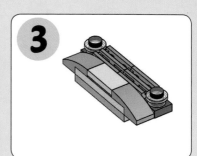

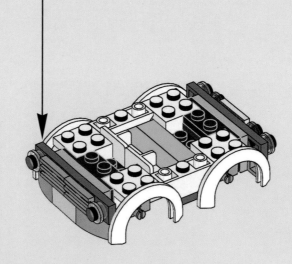

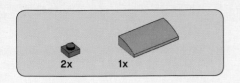

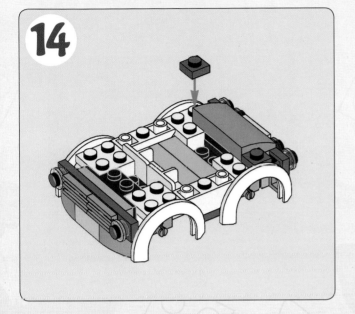

14

15

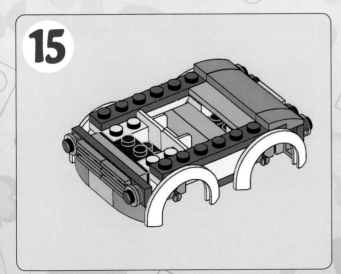

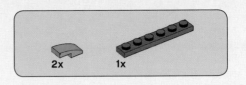

16

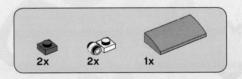

17

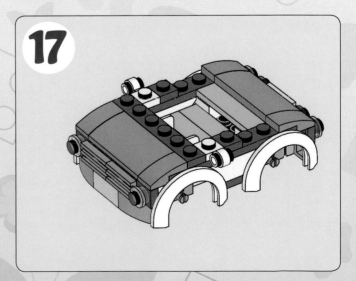

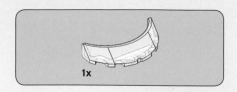

1x

18

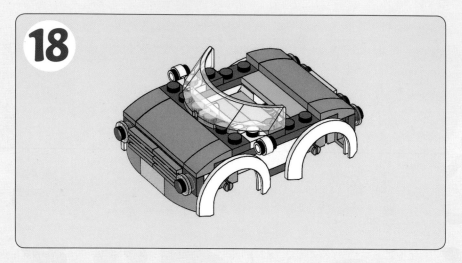

4x   4x

4x

19

Stephanie

If there's an event to plan or a party to throw, Stephanie is your girl! She is organized, full of energy, and loves to be in charge. She is a loyal and kindhearted friend, too.

Andrea

A natural perfomer, Andrea adores being center of attention and telling stories that make her friends laugh. She is a great singer and dreams of becoming a pop star someday.

Emma

Creative Emma is always making something, whether it's jewelry, fashion, art, or anything else that is beautiful! She is full of ideas and inspiration.

Meet the girls

Before setting off on a building adventure, let's meet some of Liza's friends. Liza loves to hang out with these five girls. One of them is her cousin, Mia, and the rest are Mia's closest friends. Liza is often invited to join in fun days out, events, or adventures they are planning. In the pages of this book, you'll discover more about the girls and the things they like to do in Heartlake City.

Heartlake City

Home

The girls are never bored in Heartlake City! There's so much to see and do. It's a city that's full of life, and there are all kinds of adventures to be had here.

Olivia

Science-wiz Olivia has a thirst for knowledge and loves to figure out how the world around her works. She is always inventing, building, or studying something.

Mia

Liza's cousin Mia is caring and kind. She adores animals and plans to become a vet. She is happiest outdoors, especially when she is riding her horse, Bella.

Building your own adventure

Here are some tips on building your own models.

In the pages of this book, you will discover an exciting LEGO® Friends adventure story. You will also see some clever ideas for LEGO Friends models that might inspire you to create your own. Building LEGO models from your own imagination is creative and endlessly fun. There are no limits to what you can build. This is your adventure, so jump right in and get building!

How to use this book

This book will not show you how to build the models, because it's unlikely that you'll have exactly the same bricks in your own collection. It will show you some useful build tips and model breakdowns that will help you when it comes to building your own models. Here's how the pages work...

Sometimes you'll see several different ways to build a model

What else will you build? Flashes give you even more ideas for models you could make

Special features or elements on models are annotated

Breakdowns of models feature useful build tips

Hello, I'm Tim Johnson.

Meet the builder

Tim Johnson is a LEGO fan and super-builder, and he made all the LEGO inspirational models that can be found in the pages of this book. To make the models just right for the world of LEGO Friends, Tim worked closely with the LEGO Friends team at the LEGO Group in Billund, Denmark. Use Tim's models to inspire your own amazing models.

Before you begin

Here are five handy hints to keep in mind every time you get out your bricks and prepare to build.

Organize your bricks
Organizing bricks into colors and types can save you time when you're building.

Make your model stable
Make a model that's sturdy enough to play with. You'll find useful tips for making a stable model in this book.

How nice of you to join me!

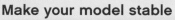

Be creative
If you don't have the perfect piece, find a creative solution! Look for a different piece that can create a similar effect.

Research
Look up pictures of what you want to build online or in books to inspire your ideas.

Have fun
Don't worry if your model goes wrong. Turn it into something else or start again. The fun is in the building!

Time to learn the lingo!

Builder talk

Did you know that LEGO builders have their own language? You will find the terms below used a lot in this book. Here's what they all mean...

Stud

Round raised bumps on top of bricks and plates are called studs. A string has a single stud at each end. Studs fit into "tubes," which are on the bottom of bricks and plates.

 2x2 corner plate

String with studs

Measurements

Builders describe the size of LEGO pieces according to the number of studs on them. If a brick has 2 studs across and 3 up, it's a 2x3 brick. If a piece is tall, it has a third number that is its height in standard bricks.

 1x1 brick

1x2 brick

2x2 brick

 2x3 brick

 1x1x5 brick

Clip

Some pieces have clips on them, into which you can fit other elements. Pieces such as ladders fasten onto bars using built-in clips.

1x1 plate with vertical clip

1x1 plate with horizontal clip

Flag with 2 clips

 Ladder with 2 clips

Hole

Bricks and plates with holes are very useful. They will hold bars or LEGO® Technic pins or connectors.

 1X1 brick with hole

 2x3 curved plate with hole

 2x2 round brick

 1x2 brick with 2 holes

 4x4 round brick

Sideways building

Sometimes you need to build in two directions. That's when you need bricks or plates like these, with studs on more than one side.

 1x4 brick with side studs

 1x1 brick with 2 side studs

 1x2/1x4 angle plate

 1x1 brick with 1 side stud

Brick

Where would a builder be without the brick? It's the basis of most models and comes in a huge variety of shapes and sizes.

2x3 curved brick

2x2 brick

1x2 brick

1x1 headlight brick

1x1 brick eye

2x2 domed brick

1x2 textured brick

1x1 round brick

Plate

Like bricks, plates have studs on top and holes on the bottom. A plate is thinner than a brick—the height of three plates is equal to one standard brick.

3x8 angled plate

1x8 plate with side rail

2x3 plate

2x2 round plate

1x2 jumper plate

1x1 tooth plate

1x1 round plate

4x4 curved plate

4x4 round plate

Tile

When you want a smooth surface to your build, you need to use a tile. Printed tiles add extra detail to your models.

1x6 tile

2x2 tile

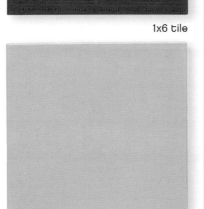
6x6 tile

2x2 tile with pin

1x2 printed tile

Slope

Slopes are bigger at the bottom than on top. Inverted slopes are the same, but upside-down. They are smaller at the bottom and bigger on top.

1x2 slope

1x2x3 inverted slope

Hinge

If you want to make a roof that opens or give a creature a tail that moves, you need a hinge. A ball joint does the same job, too.

1x2 hinge brick and 1x2 hinge plate

1x2 hinge brick and 2x2 hinge plate

Hinged plates

Ball joint socket

2x2 brick with ball joint

Hinge cylinder

1x2 plate with click hinge

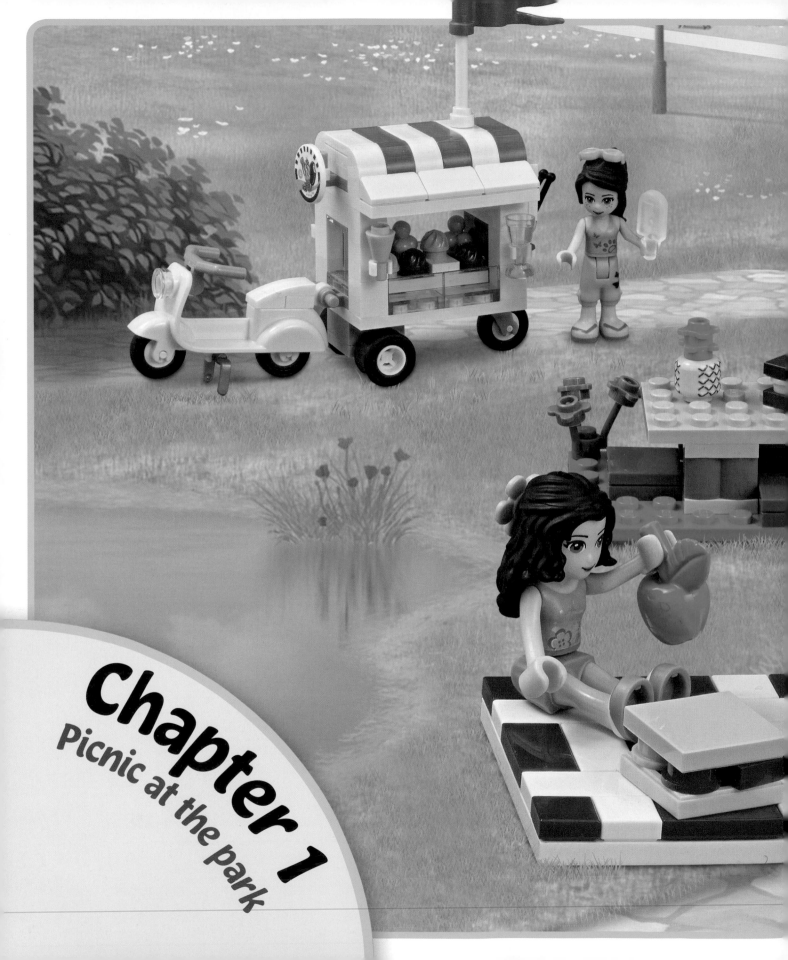

Chapter 1
Picnic at the park

Preparing a picnic

Stephanie wants to have the ultimate picnic in the park! She loves to organize events for her friends. First, she prepares sandwiches to suit every taste. Andrea lends a hand by filling up all kinds of containers with other tasty treats.

What kind of sandwich would you like?

Jars

Food can be securely packed up for a picnic in glass or plastic jars. Andrea has found lots to fill up. You only need a couple of bricks to make your own jars. Find any round-shaped brick and add a round tile or plate for the lid.

Blueberry soda

Try using two plates instead of one brick

Salad dressing

Picnic drinks

The girls will need some drinks to keep them hydrated on a hot, sunny day in Heartlake City Park. They gather up cartons and bottles of milk and orange juice for their picnic.

Top a brick with a slope to make a carton

If you don't have this printed 1x1 brick, use a plain one instead

Packing up

Andrea has started packing plastic boxes of all shapes and sizes into a picnic hamper, ready to transport to the park. The boxes' matching lids make them look like they are part of a pretty picnic set.

1x1 tile makes a square lid

Find out how to make a hamper on page 23

Sandwiches

Sandwiches are perfect for a picnic and you don't need many LEGO® pieces to make them. What fillings will yours have? Stephanie has chosen her favorite ingredients and sandwiched them between plate and tile bread slices.

2x2 slide stud makes a round bread roll

What will you build?
• Pizza slice
• Oven
• Scones
• Pie

Lettuce is a round plate

Tomato

Cheese slice

Brown bread slice

Kitchen table

Stephanie is making sandwiches for the picnic on her mom's kitchen table. It's a good job it has sturdy legs that are strong enough to hold up heaps of sandwiches. Once Stephanie gets busy making them, she can't stop! You can also find out how to build a picnic bench on pages 24–25.

Tiles make smooth top slices

Ingredients attach to studs on the bottom plate

3x3 curved plate

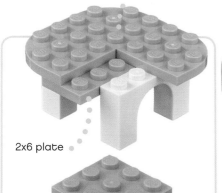

2x6 plate

Table top

Stephanie's pink table top with rounded corners is made from four 3x3 curved plates. A long, green plate holds them all together from underneath.

You only need two arch pieces to make four table legs!

Picnic equipment

Emma is gathering up picnic equipment. She has some blankets that are big enough for all the girls to sit on. Emma borrows her mom's coolers and picnic hampers, too. Luckily, the hampers have room inside for all the sandwiches Stephanie has made!

I've waited all summer to use my new picnic blanket!

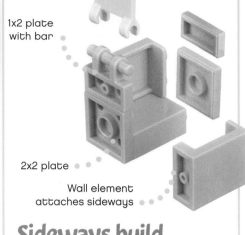

1x2 plate with bar

2x2 plate

Wall element attaches sideways

Sideways build

This cooler is built using sideways building. There are two plate pieces on their sides on the left. Everything else is built up sideways from there.

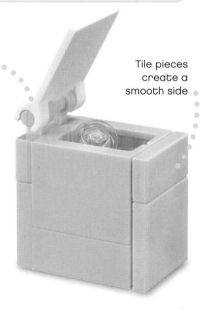

Lid opens and closes using clips

Tile pieces create a smooth side

Coolers

A cooler keeps food and drinks from getting too warm in hot weather. Emma has filled her mom's coolers with ice so the temperature inside is cold enough to keep her friends' picnic treats fresh and cool.

Angle plate

This cooler's lid connects sideways to an angle plate.

2x3 tile with clips makes a lid

Transparent round plates make ice

Temperature controls

2x3 plate

Hampers

Emma has found all kinds of hampers in her mom's collection. They all have plenty of space inside for picnic treats, and strong handles so the girls can easily carry them to the park.

This vertical bar can be held by a mini-doll

Heaps of healthy fruit

Four wall corner pieces create a square hamper

This inverted roof tile makes a good hamper base.

Handles are bar pieces

This is the same inverted roof tile that the yellow hamper uses

Picnic blanket

Emma's blankets are just about large enough for five picnicking girls, and even some of their animal friends, too! A blanket should be flat, but it could be any pattern you like: plain, stripey, spotty, or even a multi-colored plaid pattern.

Hazel, a hungry squirrel

Creating patterns

The chequered pattern on this blanket is made using different-sized tiles in contrasting colors. They all attach to a large 6x8 plate that forms the bottom layer of the blanket.

1x1 tile

1x8 tile

6x8 plate

2x2 tile

Using all the same size tiles makes a uniform pattern

Square 6x6 plate

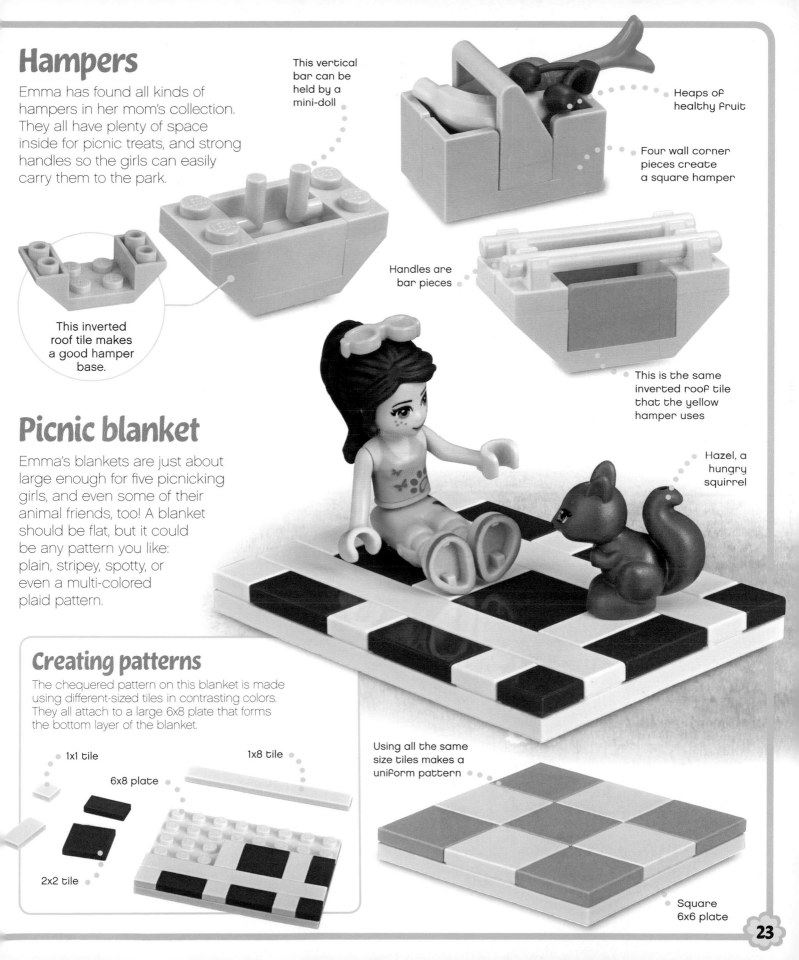

Finding a picnic spot

The girls are all prepared for their picnic so it's time to head to leafy Heartlake City Park to enjoy it. Liza drives Olivia there in her touring car. Olivia loves being outdoors. She wants to reach the park ahead of her friends so she can find them a pretty picnic spot.

I know a shady spot with a great view of the lake.

The early bird catches... a great table!

Picnic benches

The lush lawns of Heartlake City Park are filled with picnic benches. Olivia can't decide which lovely spot to choose! What kind of picnic bench could you make with your own pieces? A bench needs a flat surface and some seats.

This bench looks pretty, but is there room for all our sandwiches?

Cool water

Striped table top

1x4 plate with two studs

Smooth tile seat

Wide and sturdy legs made from an arch

Bench parts

The top part of this bench fits onto the bottom part using a 1x4 plate that only has two studs instead of four. The middle of it is smooth, like a tile. If you don't have this piece, you could use a regular 1x4 plate.

Cherry tree

Olivia knows that the best picnic spot is underneath a tree. Its branches provide cooling shade on a hot summer's day. With its wide trunk and chunky roots, this cherry tree looks like it has been growing in the park for a long time. See how to build other kinds of trees on page 62.

Cherries only grow in the summer in Heartlake City

Round plate with four bars

This round plate has four arms to attach leaves to.

Rough-textured tree trunk

Sloped bricks make thick tree roots

I guess Goldie likes pizza!

This must be the nicest spot in the park.

Goldie, the yellow warbler

If you don't have one big plate, you could use two instead

Ladybug

This bench's legs are made from a palisade brick, which looks like two logs.

Freshly cut grass

2x2 tile

2x2 plate

Add a tile on top of a plate to make a simple seat.

Picnic activities

Andrea is all about having fun! She has brought picnic games and a kite to play with at the park. After lunch, the girls spend hours skipping, kite-flying, and hoop-throwing. Once they've used up all their energy, it's time for a relaxing boat ride on the lake.

I challenge you all to a game of quoits!

Kite

Mia is running with a kite to help it catch the summer breeze. Soon it flies up, up, and (almost) away. You can make a classic kite shape with angled plates. Stephanie is keeping a firm hold on the line—a bar piece, which is the perfect size for a mini-doll hand.

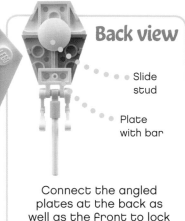

Round tile holds the angled plates together

Back view

Slide stud

Plate with bar

Connect the angled plates at the back as well as the front to lock them together securely.

2x3 angled plate

Tail, twisting in the breeze

Robot arm

1x2 plate with bar

The kite's two tails are robot arm pieces. They clip onto a plate with a bar.

Quoits

Olivia and Andrea are playing quoits. The aim of the game is to throw hoops onto spikes from a distance. A hoop on the middle spike earns you more points than if you get a hoop on one of the four outer spikes. It looks like Andrea has got this!

Spike is an antenna piece

Hoop is usually found on LEGO boats as a lifebuoy

Whirling rope

What will you build?
- Volleyball net
- Tennis racket
- Soccer goal
- Frisbee

Jump rope

"Thirty-four, thirty-five..." The girls are counting how many jumps they can make in a row. Emma is the current champion. You don't need many LEGO pieces to make a game. One string makes a jump rope!

Stud is part of the string

Swan boat

The boats in Heartlake City Park aren't just any old boats—they're graceful swan boats. With a curved neck, red bill, and long tail, this boat looks exactly like a real swan, except it has two pink seats on its back feathers!

Long neck is a curved half arch

Black 1x1 plate makes an eye

This slope and plate make a pointed bill

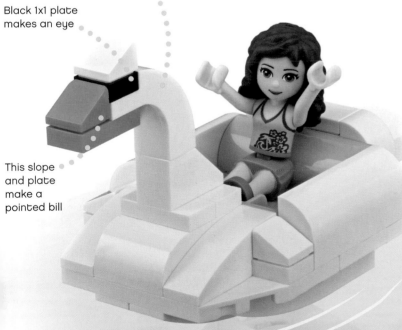

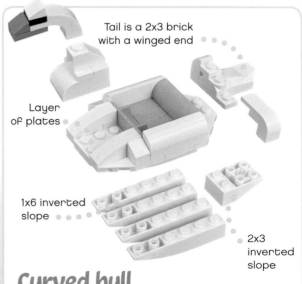

Tail is a 2x3 brick with a winged end

Layer of plates

1x6 inverted slope

2x3 inverted slope

Curved hull

A boat has a curved underside. This one is made from inverted curves. It is best to leave building this part until last, as it's not as stable to build from as the flat plate layer.

Park sights

The sun is starting to set, but there's still time to explore more of Heartlake City Park. Mia leads the girls on a leisurely stroll around some of its sights. From an ice-cream stall to a wishing bridge, there's lots to explore and many adventures to be had.

Let's go! Our day isn't over yet.

Ice-cream stall

The girls can't resist visiting this cool stall. It serves ice-cold lemonade and all kinds of ice cream. It is pulled along by a scooter, so it can move easily around the winding paths of the park and reach any picnickers in need of refreshment.

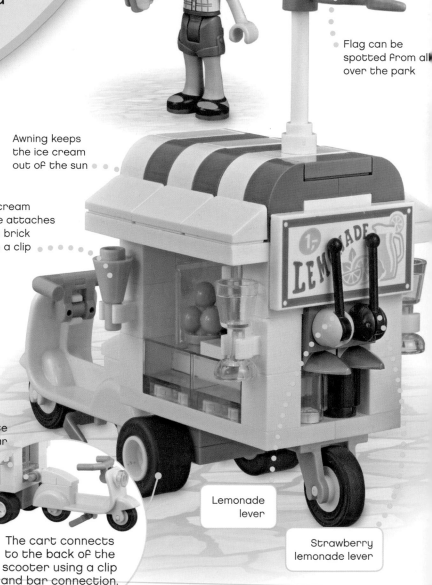

Mango ice cream

Flag can be spotted from all over the park

Awning keeps the ice cream out of the sun

Ice cream cone attaches to a brick with a clip

Lemonade lever

Strawberry lemonade lever

The cart connects to the back of the scooter using a clip and bar connection.

Plate with bar

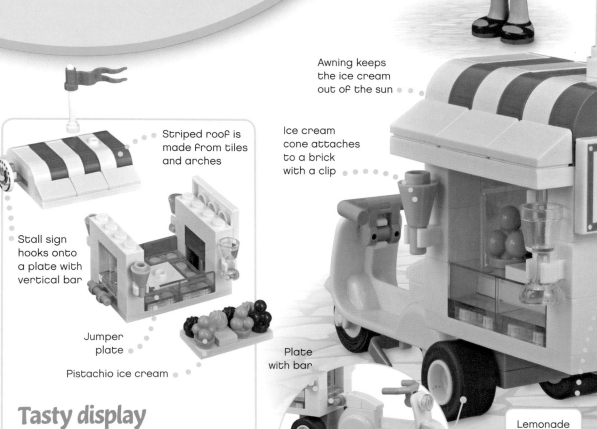

Striped roof is made from tiles and arches

Stall sign hooks onto a plate with vertical bar

Jumper plate

Pistachio ice cream

Tasty display

The stall is open on two sides, so its tempting contents can be reached easily. The ice-cream display attaches to the stall via a single stud on a jumper plate.

Wishing bridge

This wishing bridge is known as a special place in Heartlake City Park. Climb its steps, throw a coin into the gentle stream below, and make a wish. It might just come true! Emma plans to test out the wishing bridge's magic.

The gold lanterns that light up the bridge are made from four pieces.

 Tile

 Radar dish

 Round brick

 Telescope

Fences stop your mini-dolls from falling in •

River plant • • • •

Curved slopes make the steps look elegant

Riverbank

Lily pad

Green plates make grassy banks

Building bridges

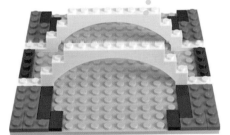

1x12x3 arched brick

Blue base plate looks like water

Two arched bricks form the base of this wishing bridge. Place the arches so they are parallel to each other on a big base plate, then arrange plates across them to make steps and a deck.

What will you build?
- Statue
- Fountain
- Park gates
- Playground

Chapter 2
The horse show

The horse course

Emma and her friends love to ride horses. They have decided to stage their own horse show for all their human and horse friends. Emma and Liza jump right into building the course for the horse show. They gather white wooden fences and hay bales to mark out a track.

We're going to put on quite a show!

What will you build?
- Show ring
- Lights
- Start gates
- Show sign

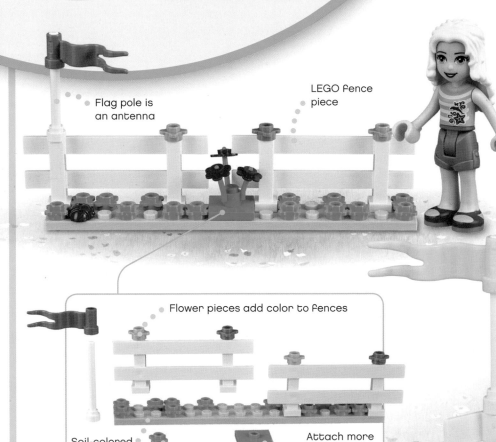

Flag pole is an antenna

LEGO fence piece

Fences

The girls can't have plain old white fences for their horse show! Liza has added flags and flowers to them. These white fence pieces come with lots of LEGO® sets, but you could also make your own using bricks for the fence posts and tiles for the wooden panels.

Flower pieces add color to fences

Soil-colored base plate

Clump of grass

Attach more flowers here

There is grass growing under these fences. It is made from green flower pieces. Adding natural details like this can bring your models to life.

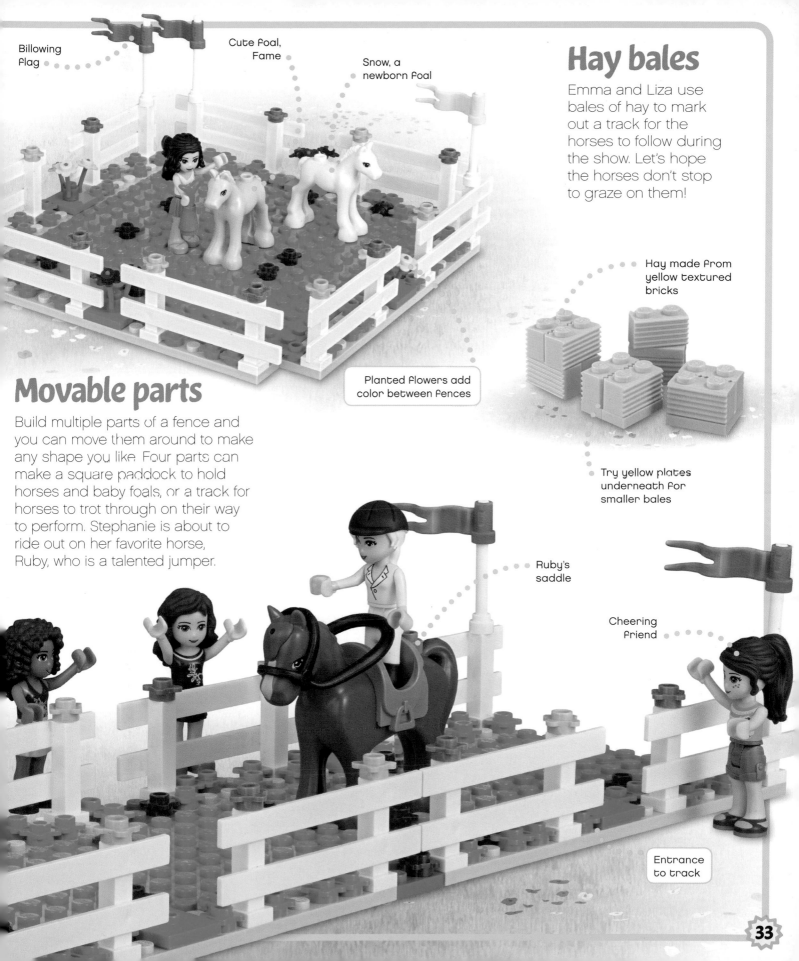

Billowing Flag

Cute foal, Fame

Snow, a newborn foal

Hay bales

Emma and Liza use bales of hay to mark out a track for the horses to follow during the show. Let's hope the horses don't stop to graze on them!

Hay made from yellow textured bricks

Planted flowers add color between fences

Try yellow plates underneath for smaller bales

Movable parts

Build multiple parts of a fence and you can move them around to make any shape you like. Four parts can make a square paddock to hold horses and baby foals, or a track for horses to trot through on their way to perform. Stephanie is about to ride out on her favorite horse, Ruby, who is a talented jumper.

Ruby's saddle

Cheering Friend

Entrance to track

The jumps

The girls have made a creative course for their horse show. There are four different jumps that will test out their horses' agility. To take first place in the horse show, the horses must clear the jumps without knocking anything off them—all within just five minutes!

These jumps will be a challenge.

Arch jump

There is lots for the horses to avoid on this jump. It has long flags, a high arch, and a round pool of water underneath. The three tiles along the top of the arch make it smooth so horses can't stumble over any studs.

Flag color matches the jump

1x2 tile

1x8 arch makes a jump wide enough for a LEGO horse

Pool of water is a blue round plate

These bricks look like a ready-made brick wall, but ordinary bricks will do, too

Fall foliage

Grass-green base plate

Brush fence jump

A horse must jump clear over foliage and flowers to get full marks on this brush fence jump. It should also stay within the tall brick walls on either side of the thick brush.

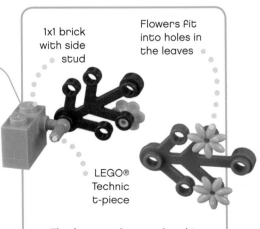

1x1 brick with side stud

Flowers fit into holes in the leaves

LEGO® Technic t-piece

The leaves that make this bushy brush fix onto a LEGO Technic t-piece, which plugs sideways into a brick with a side stud in the wall.

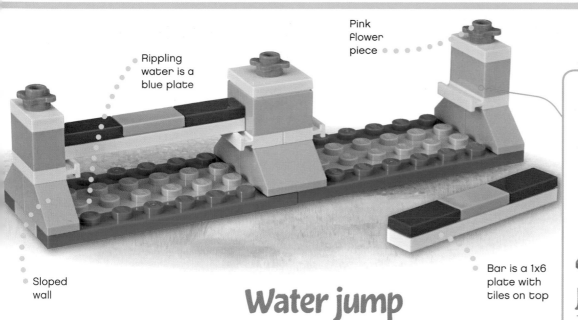

Rippling
water is a
blue plate

Pink
Flower
piece

Jumper
plate

1x2 plate
with rail

Sloped
wall

Bar is a 1x6
plate with
tiles on top

Water jump

It looks like a horse has had some
trouble jumping clear of this tricky water
jump! One of the colorful bars has fallen
off. As well as the bars on this jump, a
horse must also jump clear of its wide
strip of water and pretty pink flowers!

Jump wall

The walls on this jump
have plates with rails built
into them. The rails stick
out of the walls so the
bars of the jump can rest
loosely on them.

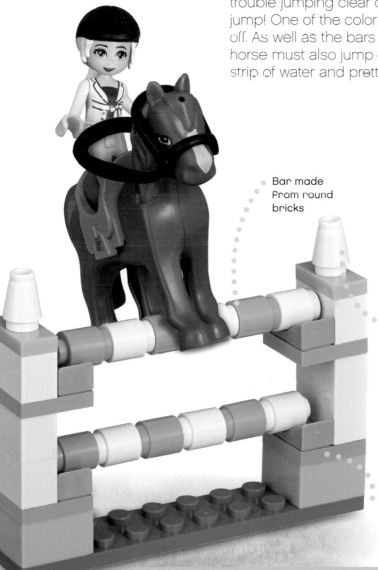

Bar made
From round
bricks

Double-bar jump

This jump is the highest on the course.
Its double bars rest loosely on grooves
in the walls on either side. It will take only
one touch from the hooves of Liza's
horse, Mocca, for both bars to topple off.

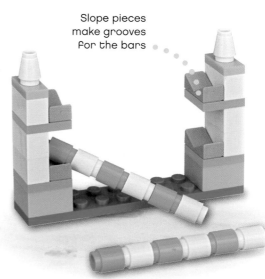

Cone pieces
make a
tapered top

Slope pieces
make grooves
for the bars

Wide plate
makes a shelf
For the bar
to rest on

Preparing the horses

Emma and her horse, Robin, are next up in the horse show and they're almost ready to perform. Emma is helping Robin to look his best for the show by using a washing station. There are no points for appearance in the horse show, but the horses do like to make an effort.

Robin will be pearly white when I'm finished.

Washing station

Emma is working hard to get Robin sparkling! She rubs soap into his soft coat, mane, and tail, then washes off the bubbly lather with a powerful water jet. Next, Robin plans to get up his energy levels for the show by crunching on a carrot from the washing station's trough.

Freshly picked carrot

Grooming equipment

Working walls

The walls of the washing station are functional. There are bricks with clips built into them for cleaning and grooming accessories. The trough is also built into the wall. It is made from two inverted slopes with wall corner pieces on top.

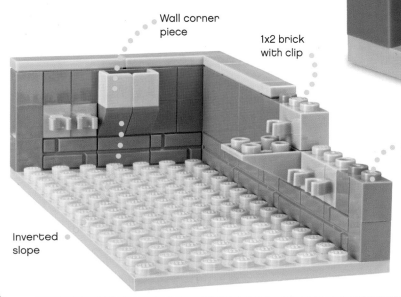

Wall corner piece

1x2 brick with clip

One-stud wide walls

Inverted slope

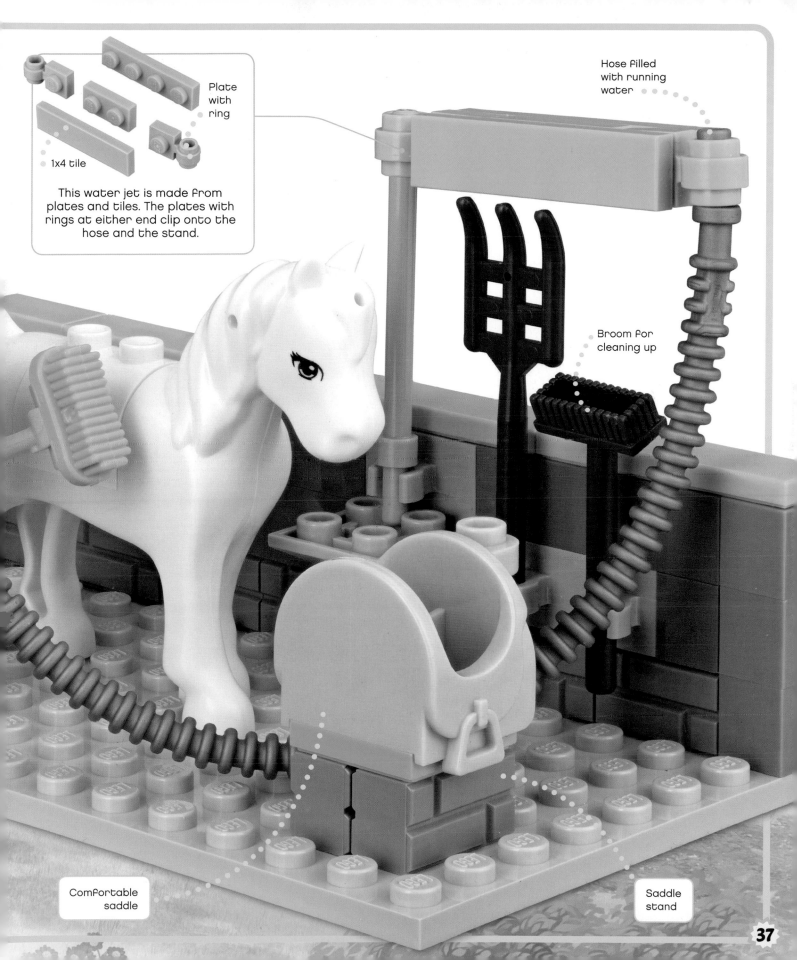

Plate with ring

1x4 tile

This water jet is made from plates and tiles. The plates with rings at either end clip onto the hose and the stand.

Hose filled with running water

Broom for cleaning up

Comfortable saddle

Saddle stand

The stands

Mia and Olivia have built colorful stands for their friends and family to watch the horse show from. Every seat has a good view of the track. The crowd cheers from the stands as Stephanie and Ruby and Emma and Robin proudly trot into the enclosure.

Take a seat! The show is about to start.

What will you build?

- Drinks stand
- Food stall
- Riders' tent
- VIP area

Leather reins

Smile for the crowds, Ruby!

Riding helmet

Horse-show flag

Spectator stand

The excitement is building in the spectator stand at the horse show! Olivia's friends Matthew and Julian have joined her on the stand. Julian is the offical photographer at the horse show. He is running up and down the stand's steps to get the best angles.

Cones and plates make hand rails

Barrier stops mini-dolls from falling off

Rear view

Step-by-step

These stands are built up in layers, starting from two long 1x10 bricks that form the sides of the stands. A gray brick and two plates make the start of the steps, then a pink plate forms the first layer of the seats. Three long tiles on top of the pink plate make smooth seats. Exposed studs aren't very comfortable!

4x10 plate

1x10 brick

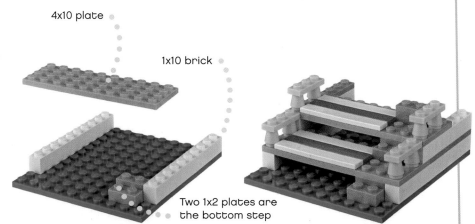

Two 1x2 plates are the bottom step

The prizes

The judges' scores are in at the horse show, and the winner is announced on the score board. The winner is... Stephanie! Olivia takes the gleaming silver winner's trophy from its case and presents it to Stephanie and her champion horse, Ruby, as they both beam with pride.

It's the taking part that counts. Yeah, right!

Scoreboard

Mia has been helping the judges to mark the horses' jump times and points positions on this scoreboard. It tells everyone that Ruby has ended the show in first place. Well done, Ruby! Major took second place.

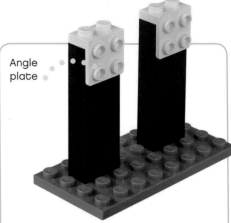

Angle plate

The scoreboard is made from a plate that attaches sideways to angle plates. They sit on top of posts made from bricks.

Stickered tile

Jumper plate

Marks out of five for a horse's performance

Clock records finishing times

The names, numbers, and flowers on this scoreboard attach sideways to jumper plates.

RUBY

MAJOR

Gleaming glass

These transparent pieces look like a sparkling glass case. The sides are wall elements. They are held together at the top and bottom with transparent ring plates.

Top ring plate

Wall element

Trophy case

A special trophy needs a special trophy case. This one is clear on all sides so everyone at the horse show can catch a glimpse of the shining silver winners' trophy it holds. The trophy stands on a base that is decorated with horse show symbols.

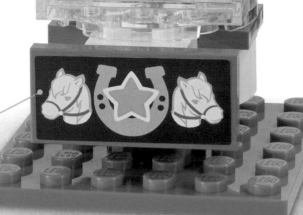

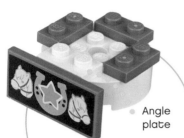

Angle plate

The stickered tile attaches sideways to an angle plate.

You're the star jumper, Stephanie.

Ruby was the one doing all the jumping!

What will you build?

- Winners' podium
- Judges' table
- Rosettes
- Prizes

Chapter 3
Heartlake City carnival

Ready to rock

It's carnival day in Heartlake City! In just a few hours, the girls will play their musical instruments on top of a parade float that will travel all around their city. They will entertain crowds of people, so the girls are practicing hard!

One, two, a-one, two, three, four...

Stephanie's LEGO® guitar adds strings to this band!

We can do this, band members!

Drum kit

Mia is the drummer in the band. It's important that she plays her part right, as the other girls must keep to the beat she sets. Mia's drum kit has three drums and two cymbals, which she strikes in a steady rhythm using two drumsticks.

Hinged plate holds the cymbal at an angle, ready for Mia to crash!

A radar dish attached to a bar makes a cymbal

Bars make good drumsticks

A telescope piece holds up this drum

If you don't have this special printed tile, use a plain one

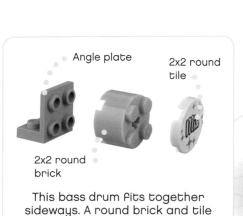

Angle plate

2x2 round tile

2x2 round brick

This bass drum fits together sideways. A round brick and tile attach to an angle plate.

Piano

Olivia plays the piano keyboard. It's just the right height for her to play comfortably when she's standing (and sometimes dancing). She presses down on its white keys to play the band's tunes.

Keyboard

2x2 tile

1x6 plate

1x2 grille

The keyboard on Mia's piano is built up in three layers. The first is all black plates. The second is a narrow plate and white grille pieces that make long keys. Smooth tiles make a shiny top layer that leaves most of the keys clear.

What will you build?

- Saxophone
- Double bass
- Harmonica
- Violin

Wall element holds up the keyboard

A plate makes a sturdy base

Microphone clips into a robot arm piece

Microphone stand is a bar and a cone

Andrea's raised platform has two studs for her feet and one for her microphone.

Andrea stands here

Jumper plate with one stud

Microphone

Andrea is a natural performer and she loves to sing. Heartlake City Carnival is her chance to shine! She adjusts the microphone to just the right height to capture her beautiful singing voice.

Circular plate puts Andrea in the spotlight

Drive time

Emma isn't part of the carnival band, but she's come along to drive the tractor that tows her friends' float along. She hooks the float to the back of the tractor and settles into the drivers' seat. The girls' float is ready to join the parade!

I've always wanted to drive a tractor!

Tractor

This tractor's big back wheels pack enough power to let it tow along the girls' bright float during the parade. Tractors aren't known for reaching fast speeds, but that doesn't matter. The parade moves at a gentle pace so there's plenty of time for the crowds to enjoy the girls' musical entertainment!

Carnival flowers

Angle plate

Chair

Mud guards

There are so many creative ways to use your LEGO pieces. A chair piece is a mud guard on this tractor. It connects sideways to the body of the tractor with an angle plate.

Step onto the tractor here

MF ✿ 034

Transparent round plates are headlights

Smaller front wheel

Tailpipe

Towbar connection

It's important that the towbar piece on the float is the same height as the connection on the vehicle, so that the tractor can pull the float along easily.

What will you build?

- Truck
- Themed stage
- Road
- Warehouse

Ready to roll

Band practice is over and it's time for the girls to take to their parade float stage. Stephanie takes charge of checking that all instruments are in the right places, and the loud-speaker system is set up correctly, ready to boom the girls' music all across the city.

Testing... Can you hear me, Heartlake City?

Parade float

Carnivals are all about celebrating and having fun, so a parade float should be as bright and colorful as you can make it. The girls' vibrant float has space for the entire band. It also needs wheels and a place where the float can attach to a vehicle, so it can roll along in the parade.

Speakers

An awesome band needs a state-of-the-art loudspeaker system! These two tall speaker stands fit onto the parade float and blast out the girls' music far and wide.

This plate with a vertical clip connects the speaker to the stand.

Towbar attaches to a vehicle

Radar dish makes a wide speaker

Antenna makes a speaker stand

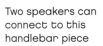

Two speakers can connect to this handlebar piece

Arch pieces look pretty and act as wheel trims, too

Wild wheels

To make a parade float, it's best to start with the stage first, then add the wheels. Otherwise you might find your float floats away as you build! The wheel section on this float is built separately from the stage. The wheels and platform supports are built on top of one long, pink plate that creates a sturdy base.

2x14 plate

Plates support the platform

Jumper plate

Attach jumper plates anywhere on the stage for equipment to attach to.

Rounded corner plates make a curved edge for the float

1x2 brick with hole

LEGO Technic pin

The thick wheels attach to the base plate with a LEGO® Technic pin and a brick with a hole.

Colorful flowers attach to sideways-facing bricks built into the float.

Flower piece

49

Parade preparations

The girls' float might be ready for the parade, but the girls themselves aren't yet! The girls have been working hard at band rehearsal and preparing their float. They hurry away to a dressing room to freshen up before their Heartlake City Carnival debut.

Just a quick tidy-up, then it's time to hit the stage.

Dressing screen

This striped dressing screen is just the right height for a mini-doll to change behind. It's made from three separate panels that can fold into any shape that works well in a room. The girls take turns to get spruced-up behind it, while Maxie the cat purrs his approval.

Comb

Hairdryer

Mirror

This swiveling full-length mirror is also multi-functional. It has built-in storage for hairbrushes and hairdryers, so any equipment the girls might need while they're getting dressed is just a mini-doll arm's length away!

Brick with clip built into the back

The mirror's base is a turntable piece, which allows it to spin.

This mirror sticker is stuck on the side of one, tall 1x2x6 brick

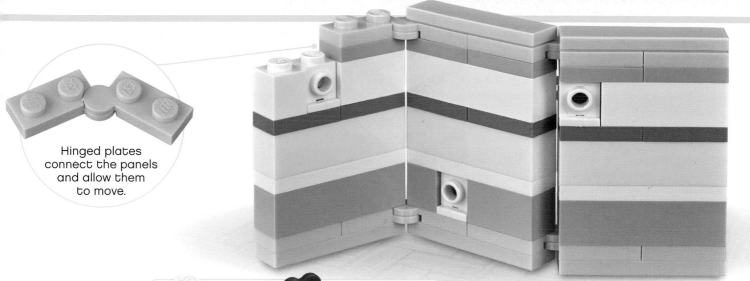

Hinged plates connect the panels and allow them to move.

Rear view

Headlight brick

Heart fits onto Flower

The studs on decorative pieces like the yellow flower fit into the back of headlight bricks.

Alternate bricks and plates to make different-sized stripes

Each panel is built upwards, like a wall

Friendly cat, Maxie

Meet the crowds

Barriers have gone up on the streets of Heartlake City and crowds of people have flocked behind them to watch the parade. A camera crew arrives to capture the action, too. The girls smile for the cameras and greet the crowds with horns and lanterns.

This carnival crowd is electric!

Mouthpiece is a LEGO Technic t-piece

Horn is a cone piece

Horn

Carnivals are all about having fun, so they're great places to make lots of noise! Andrea is giving this carnival horn a test-honk before handing it out to the crowd.

Camera lens is a transparent round plate

Microphone is a globe piece

Movie reel print on a tile

1x2 brick with side studs and stand

Nozzle piece

The handle on this camera is a LEGO nozzle, often found at the end of hoses! The top of it plugs into an open stud on the brick above it.

Cameras

The girls' school teacher Ms. Stevens and their friend Matthew are recording the parade on video cameras. They're going to report on it for the school website.

A yellow round brick lights up this lantern

Fiery glow is an orange round plate

Lantern handle is an upturned goblet

Lanterns

The parade takes place as night falls in Heartlake City. Emma and Olivia hand out glowing lanterns to the crowds to light up the city streets.

What will you build?
- Ferris wheel
- Fairy lights
- Carnival flags
- Fireworks

Here comes the girls' float!

Connected barriers are ladder pieces with two clips

Plates with vertical clips hold up the barrier

Barriers

These metal barriers are rolled out for big events in Heartlake City. They show excited crowds where to stand and cheer—and also stop them from getting too excited and running out into the parade route! Flowers on the barriers add even more color to the carnival environment.

Colorful flowers attach to the barrier bars via a plate with clip piece.

Chapter 4
Adventure weekend

At the campsite

It's set to be a beautiful weekend, so nature-loving Olivia has organized an outdoor adventure with her friends. They have all headed out to the woods on the outskirts of the city. Olivia has hired a camping hut on a scenic campsite.

I know a pretty place with comfy beds!

What will you build?
- Bicycle rack
- Camping chairs
- Camping stove
- Tents

Camping hut

Olivia knows this pretty camping hut is much more comfortable than a tent! There are home comforts like beds and electricity, and cheery flowers on the windowsill. It looks like Oscar the hedgehog wants to come inside, too!

Hanging lantern

Window box with flowers

Oscar, the hedgehog

Door handle

56

Lamp • •   • Cellphone

Magazine
• stand

• Drawers

Adding furniture to
your hut will bring
it to life.

1x2 tile

• Sliding stud

1x4 plate
with click
hinge

1x2 plate with
click hinge

Bunk bed

The bunk bed clips
onto plates with click
hinges that are built
into the wall. Sliding
stud pieces under
the plates lock them
together. The top
layer of tiles is the
pillow and sheets.

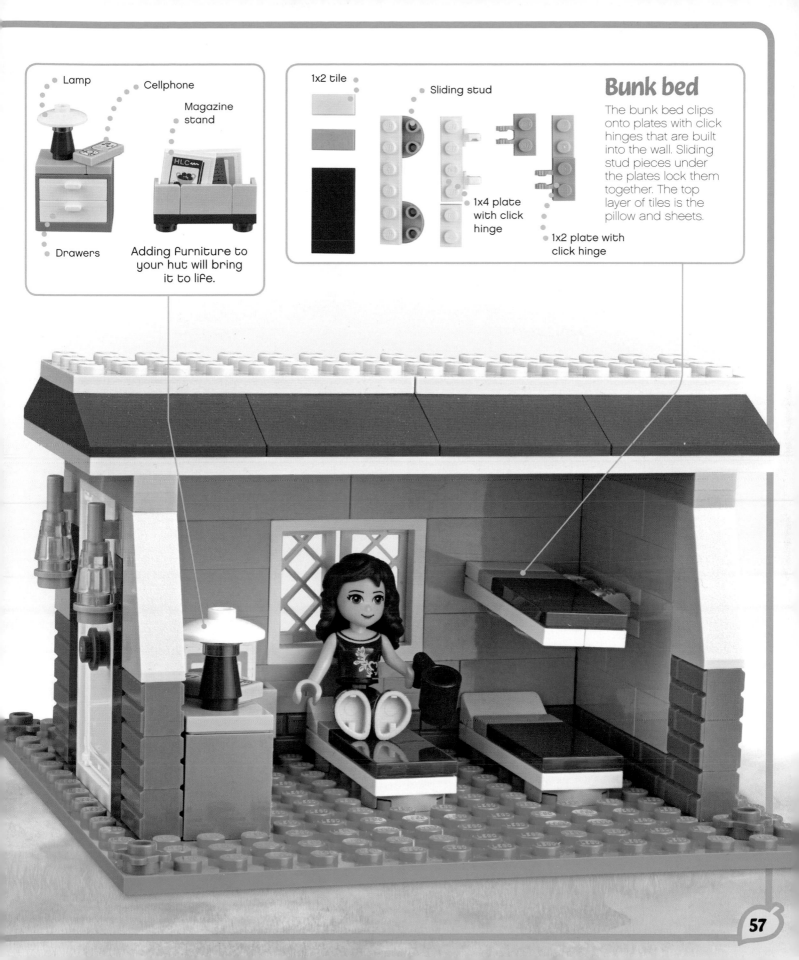

Around the campfire

It's the end of the first day of the girls' adventure weekend and they're really starting to settle in. After saying hello to their squirrel neighbors, they light up lanterns and a cozy campfire as night begins to fall on the campsite.

Gather round for dinner!

Campfire

The girls are feeling hungry, so Stephanie is cooking up a hearty dinner for them all on the campfire. Once it's ready, the girls can gather on the wooden seats around it and enjoy their dinner together.

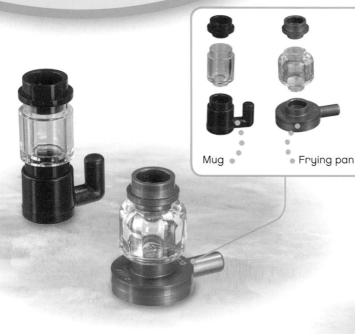

The bases of these lanterns are made from an upside-down frying pan and mug!

Mug

Frying pan

Plate filled with tasty salad

Lanterns

There aren't many lights on the campsite, so the girls use camping lanterns to help them find their way around in the dark.

Two slope
bricks make
a tiny roof

Fire piece

This 1x1
slope looks
like solid
rock!

4x4
round
plate

Start a fire

It's easier to make a LEGO®
campfire than it is to make a real
one! This one is built up from a
round plate. Gray bricks make a
rocky base, and orange and brown
bricks make fire and firewood.

Squirrel house

This squirrel lives in a wooden
tree house on the campsite.
It can see everyone who
comes and goes from its
lofty perch!

Flower
decorations

Squirrel perch is
a jumper plate

1x4 arch
brick

2x2 corner
plate

Palisade
brick

Cozy home

The walls on this squirrel house
are made from palisade bricks.
There's a line of plates over
them that makes the house
look even prettier. Arches on
the next layer leave room for
the squirrel's pointy ears!

Roaring flame

Firewood

Burning embers

Stacked-up plates
and a tile make a
wooden seat

Campsite facilities

Time to get washed and dressed for the day.

It's a new day on the campsite and the girls wake up to the sounds of the birds and animals that live in the woods. Liza and Mia head to the campsite's facilities before breakfast so they can use them before their fellow campers beat them to it!

Shower block

The shower block has all the facilities that campers might need to prepare for a day in the great outdoors. There are two powerful showers to get washed under. Liza is combing her hair in front of the dressing table mirror.

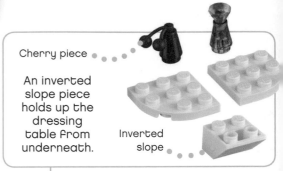

Cherry piece

An inverted slope piece holds up the dressing table from underneath.

Inverted slope

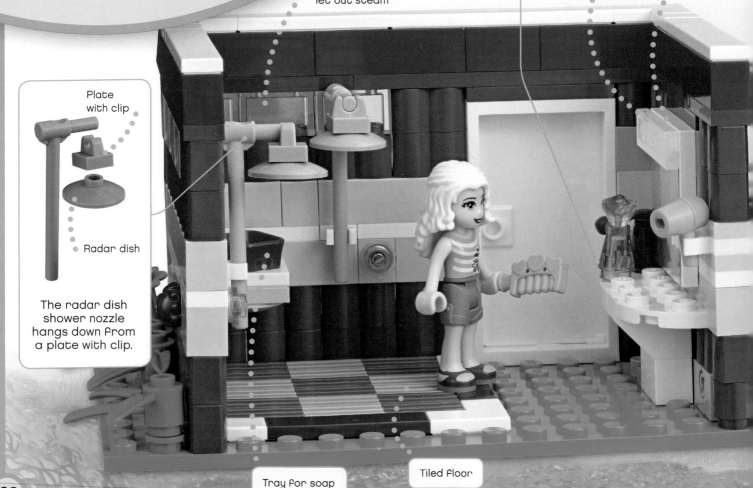

High windows to let out steam

Light for mirror

Mirror attached to wall

Plate with clip

Radar dish

The radar dish shower nozzle hangs down from a plate with clip.

Tray for soap

Tiled floor

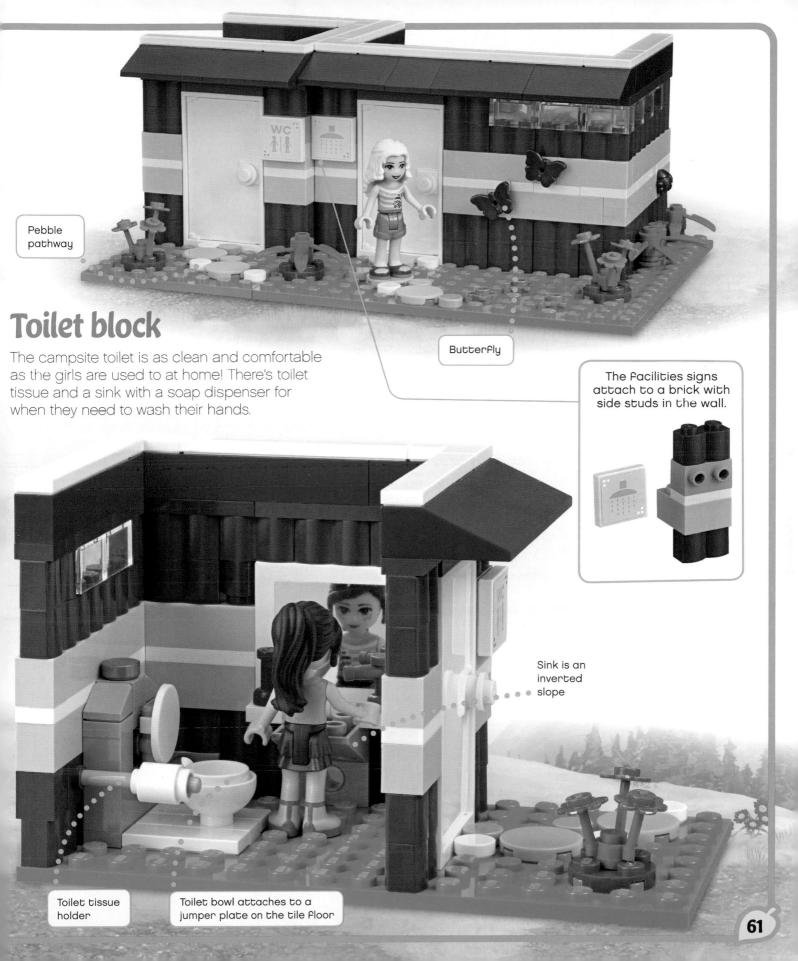

Pebble
pathway

Butterfly

Toilet block

The campsite toilet is as clean and comfortable as the girls are used to at home! There's toilet tissue and a sink with a soap dispenser for when they need to wash their hands.

The facilities signs attach to a brick with side studs in the wall.

Sink is an inverted slope

Toilet tissue holder

Toilet bowl attaches to a jumper plate on the tile floor

WC

61

Into the woods

The girls are going on a nature trail. Emma has planned out the route to make sure her friends visit all the most beautiful and interesting spots in the woods. They hike through thick woodland to a cave, meeting all kinds of wildlife along the way.

I'll capture the beautiful scenery on my camera.

Trees

There are many different varieties of trees in the woods. Some have budding flowers, others have vibrant leaves. Emma sees them all as a photo opportunity!

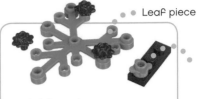

Leaf piece

1x3 plate

Adding plates on top of foliage stops them from falling off the tree.

Blossom

Fall leaf

Hanging branch

Cream, the rabbit

Plates in a cross shape

Half arch

Sturdy trunk

The slope and arch pieces that this tree trunk is made from are held together at the top using a layer of plates. This makes the model stable enough to play with.

Cave

The girls follow Emma's trail up to a cave. They feel a little scared when they look through its jagged opening to the cave's dark interior, but there's no reason to be. This is a meeting place for many of the woodland animals!

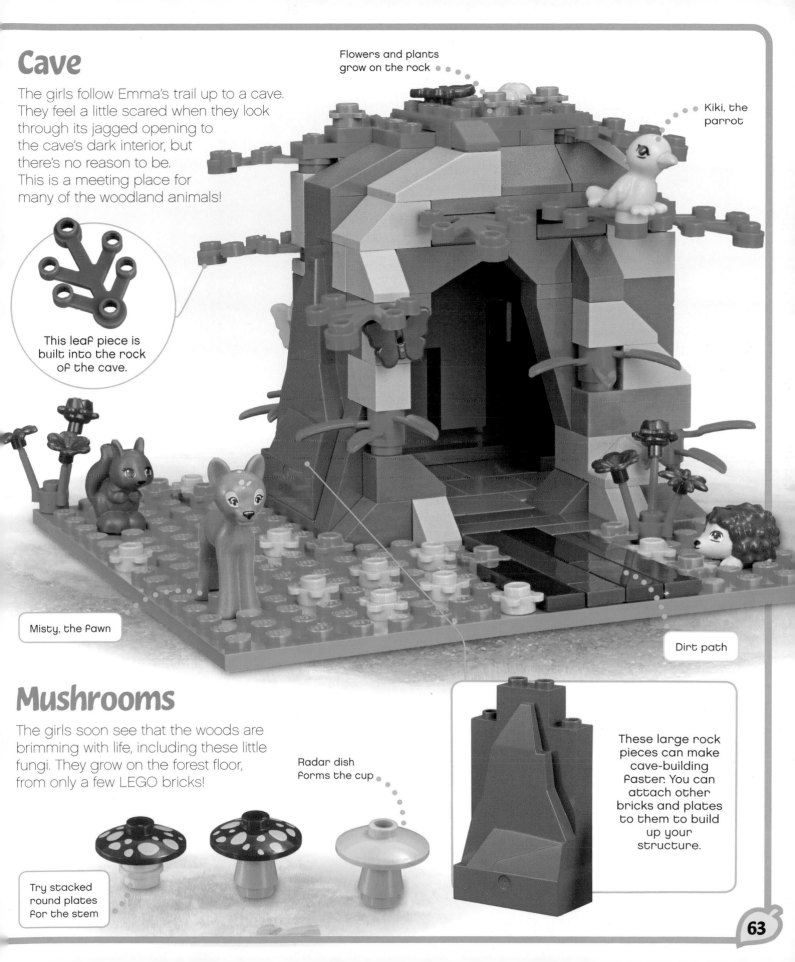

Flowers and plants grow on the rock

Kiki, the parrot

This leaf piece is built into the rock of the cave.

Misty, the fawn

Dirt path

Mushrooms

The girls soon see that the woods are brimming with life, including these little fungi. They grow on the forest floor, from only a few LEGO bricks!

Radar dish forms the cup

These large rock pieces can make cave-building faster. You can attach other bricks and plates to them to build up your structure.

Try stacked round plates for the stem

The waterfall

The girls have been climbing uphill for hours, but they realize that their efforts were all worth it when they eventually arrive at this majestic waterfall. It's the final spot on Olivia's nature trail, and the perfect place to relax after a tiring day of woodland exploration.

Hiking is amazing, but exhausting!

Jagged rockface is made like the cave on page 63

Falling water

There is a wall made from plates in white and shades of blue behind the transparent blue bricks of the waterfall. This makes the water look more natural.

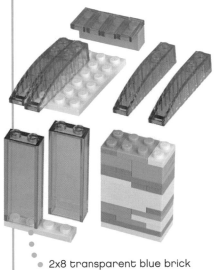

● 2x8 transparent blue brick

Waterfall

The fast-flowing waters of this waterfall run over a sheer drop at the top of tall rocks. The water splashes down into a bubbling pool below, where Bubbles the turtle is taking a cooling dip.

Curved slopes
look like flowing
water

Bubbles,
the turtle

Transparent
round plates make
bubbling water

**What will
you build?**
• Visitor center
• Tree house
• Trail signs
• Lake

Chapter 5
surprise party

Party planning

Can you keep a secret? The girls are planning a surprise party for Liza! It's to say thank you for all the great trips they've had in her touring car. The girls all want it to be perfect, so they pay an advance visit to the venue to check out all the cool things it has to offer.

Shh! Don't tell Liza what we've got planned!

One record plays here while DJ Stephanie readies the next one, opposite

I can't wait until it's time to party!

Dancefloor

Andrea loves a brightly lit dancefloor, because she can see what everyone's feet are doing! She chose her shoes for the party especially to match the colors of this one!

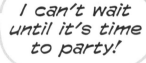

Checkered floor is a mix of jumper plates and tiles on an 8x8 plate

DJ set

Every party needs music, and Stephanie is picking all the tunes at this one! Her record collection is made of 2x2 round tiles, played on a high-tech DJ console with separate speakers on either side.

Start your DJ set with a 2x8 plate

Use 1x1 round bricks and 2x2 round plates to make the legs

Headlight brick

1x2 brick with hole

A 2x4 angle plate attaches under the DJ set so this funky stickered tile can be added sideways.

Speakers

Two headlight bricks and a 1x2 LEGO® Technic brick with a hole make a good loudspeaker. Use sideways building to add a grille and a radar dish piece.

Disco lights

These groovy lights are sure to get the party started. With different colors on five sides of a 1x1 brick with side studs, they're a really bright idea!

It doesn't matter what colors you use for disco lights

A 2x4 jumper plate gives the lights a stable base.

Fun and games

This party is going to have everything! Emma has put her design skills into action to decorate the venue and inventive Olivia has made a brightly colored piñata. With Mia busy adding balloons into the mix, everything is starting to feel very festive!

Preparing is almost as much fun as a party!

Bunting

Pretty bunting brightens any event, and for Liza's surprise party Emma has made a beautiful string of flags and flowers. Best of all, they can be attached to anything!

A mix of 1x1 plates and flowers adds variety. Attach them using plates with clips.

A curved slope holds the bunting in place

I know Liza will love these pretty colors!

This string has studs at both ends and notches along its length

Attach a tall brick to a wide plate to make a steady support for your bunting

Use antennae of different lengths to secure your balloons to jumper plates

What will you build?
• Pass the parcel
• Musical chairs
• Photo booth
• Gift table

Balloons

A party with plenty of balloons is sure to go with a bang! You can mix domed bricks and inverted dome bricks to make them, as both can be attached to axles and antenna no matter which way up they are.

Connect two dome pieces with an axle to make this smooth round shape.

String with studs

The more colors a piñata has, the better

Piñata

A paper piñata full of treats is a fun way to share party goodies. Everyone takes turns trying to break it open, until the contents fall out for everyone to enjoy.

Party equipment

Stephanie is a seasoned party planner. She has started to think about the food menu for the party. Any good party has good party snacks! Stephanie has found a buffet counter and serving tables at the party venue, and she's full of ideas about how she'll fill them.

I've found everything we need!

Lazy Susan

This spinning table is known as a Lazy Susan. It makes reaching food easy. Rotate the table top and the food comes to you! This handy table is Stephanie's favorite find of the day.

A round brick makes a sturdy center

A round plate with four studs makes a smooth table top

A turntable piece at the base of the Lazy Susan makes it spin.

Turntable piece

Alternating tile colors makes a striped tabletop

These rounded table legs are made from a mudguard piece, often found on LEGO® car models

There's a 4x8 plate under the tile pieces

Bench

Stephanie thinks this long bench is the perfect place to display the many tarts and cakes that she plans to bake for the party (find them on pages 76 and 77). Its colorful striped table top and funky pink legs are perfect for a party.

Hot buffet

The party guests will have to get in line for this delicious buffet! The hot buffet stand has three display compartments that keep different foods separate, and glowing heat lamps that keep its contents warm.

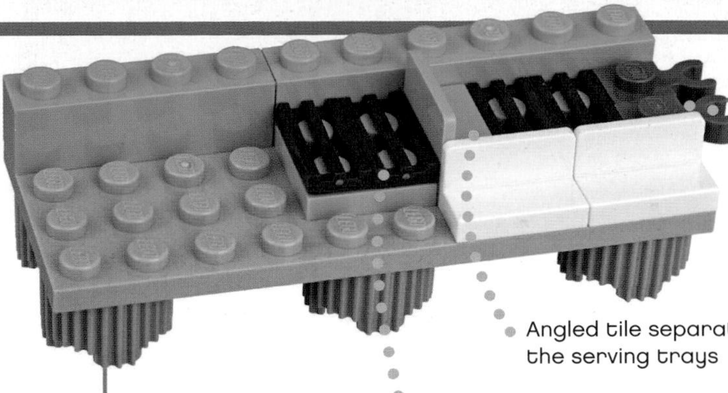

Plate with clip for serving utensils to attach to

Angled tile separates the serving trays

Red grille piece

Hidden heat

It's the little details that can make your models extra special! There are red grille pieces under the display trays on the hot buffet stand. They look like a hot grill that's keeping the food toasty from underneath!

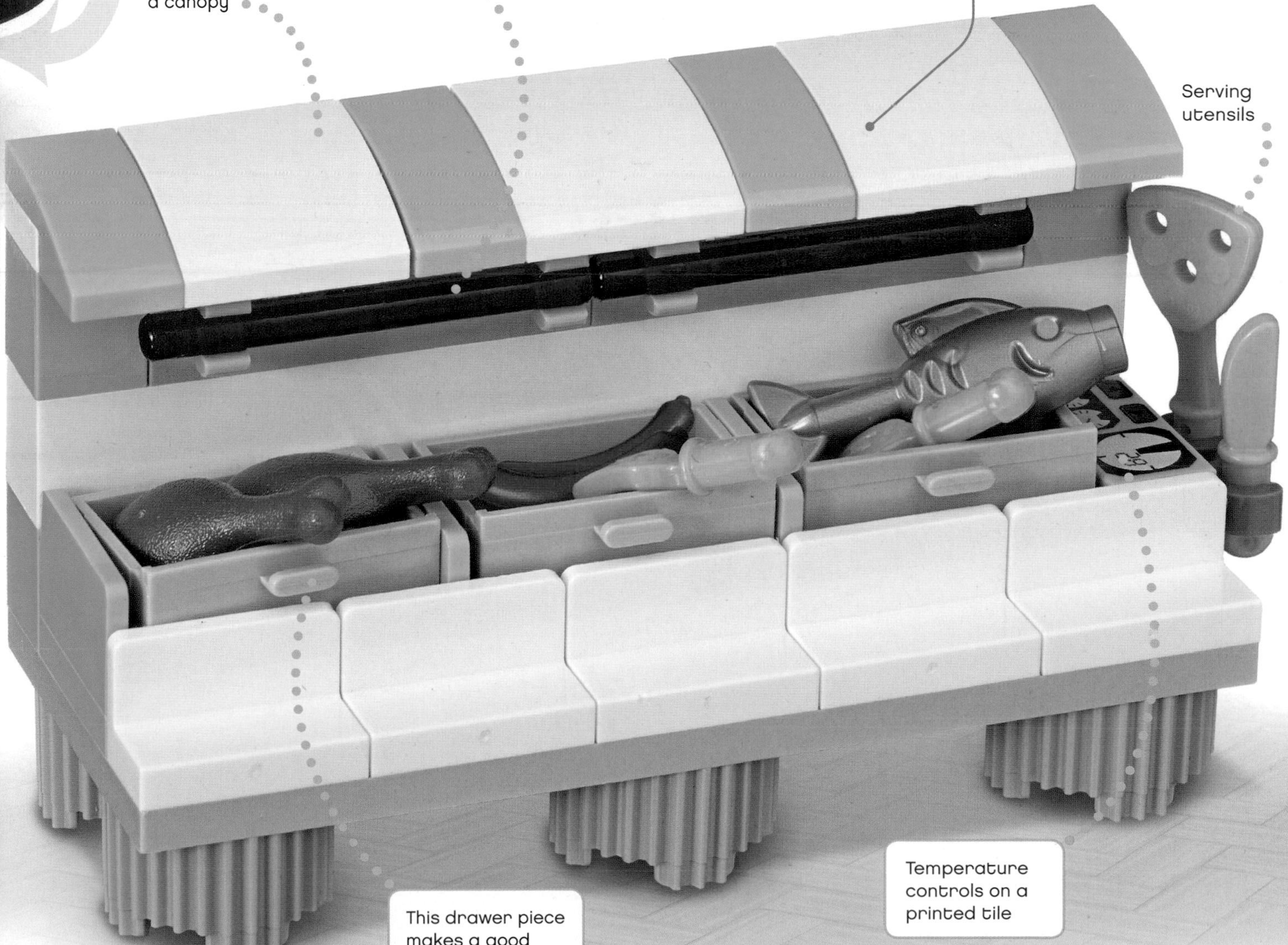

Curved slopes make a canopy

This heat lamp is a lightsaber piece, found in many LEGO® *Star Wars*® sets

Serving utensils

This drawer piece makes a good serving tray

Temperature controls on a printed tile

Party food and drinks

Olivia knows the clock is ticking. Liza is due to arrive at the party venue in just a matter of hours and the girls haven't set up the food yet! It's all hands on deck under Stephanie's leadership to finish preparing the party before the guests arrive.

Need a job to do? Ask Stephanie!

Bread basket

If you don't have ready-made bread pieces, make some yourself using jumper plates in shades of bread! Make a box for them all and you have a bread basket.

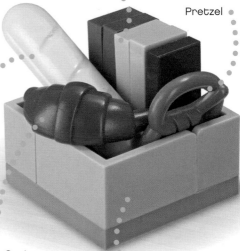

Stacking jumper plates at an angle makes natural-looking bread slices

Pretzel

Baguette

Croissant

Box made from wall corner pieces with a plate underneath

Blade is a crowbar piece, often used by LEGO burglers!

A tile on a plate makes a block of cheese

Cheese cutter

Stephanie is testing out this cool cheese cutter. Its sharp blade cuts through the block of cheese, making a perfect slice. Stephanie thinks it's best that she tests out the cheese, too. Yum!

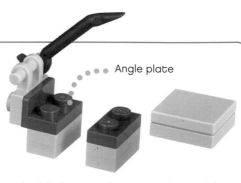

Angle plate

The blade attaches to a plate with bar, which fits sideways to an angle plate built into the cutter.

Cheese slice is one yellow tile

Healthy snacks

The girls have prepared bowls of healthy snacks for the party. There's a salad bowl filled with all kinds of crisp leaves along with handy salad servers. The overflowing fruit bowl is made from a dome and a plate.

This rock crystal piece becomes breadsticks!

This blue flower piece makes a decorative salad bowl.

Dips and chips

Dips and tortilla chips are perfect for sharing at a party. This box holds three flavors of tasty dips, as well as vegetable sticks and breadsticks to dip into them.

Tortilla chip is a 1x1 slope piece

Drinks

The girls aren't sure what kind of juice their guests will want to drink at their party, so they've made every flavor they can think of! There's water, too, to keep everyone hydrated after hitting the dancefloor.

Ice cube

1x4 brick with three holes

Dip tip

Ordinary bricks can be used in many different ways. These dipping items fit perfectly into the studs of the brick with three holes that forms the back part of the box.

Water bottle made from a round brick, cone, and round plate lid

A yellow globe piece on a round brick makes apple juice!

Try using stacked round plates

Ice bucket made from a radar dish

Dessert table

The party food and drinks are set up, now all the girls need are some desserts. Not many people know this, but Liza has a sweet tooth. Liza's cousin Mia knows that any party for Liza must have heaps of sweet treats! Luckily, all the girls have baked... a lot!

This is one sweet party! Hope Liza likes our treats.

Mille-feuille

These sweet little pastries are a French dessert. Emma took great care when she was piping the striped icing onto them! They're so pretty, the girls have set up a display table just for mille-feuille.

Lemon icing is a grille piece

Layers of pastry are stacked 1x2 plates

Using plates (with studs to attach things to) on a table top can prevent whatever you put on it from falling off.

This flower looks like a cherry on top!

Swirly chocolate icing

This flower piece looks like pink icing

Tiny treats

The girls didn't need long to make these dainty jellies and cakes. They're made from just two or three pieces each. Find some tasty-looking colors and get baking/ building some for the party!

Smooth tiles make smooth icing

Use transparent pieces to make jelly

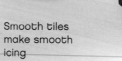

Desserts

These larger desserts are the stuff of Liza's dreams! There's all kinds of tarts, pies, and cookies here. Some are ready-made LEGO pieces, but if you don't have them, build your own with any pieces you can find.

Round tile makes the top layer of a cake

1x1 round plates make this strawberry filling

What will you build?
- Chocolate fountain
- Hot chocolate
- Candy
- Popcorn

Cookie pieces

The more cake layers, the better for Liza!

A transparent sliding stud piece makes a jelly filling for a tart

Cake stand

Liza is sure to visit this cake stand at the party! It has two layers for displaying tiny treats. It can stand up on its own or form the centerpiece of the girls' dessert table.

2x2 round plate

Antenna

Jumper plate

Layered cakes

The cake stand has a jumper plate base, which an antenna piece connects to to make the center of the stand. Round plates with holes form the two tiers.

Surprise!

Liza can't believe the girls have thrown a party for her—and it's the coolest party in Heartlake City! Stephanie cranks up the music to get the party started. It's time for the girls to celebrate!

 Penguin Random House

Senior Editor Hannah Dolan
Additional Editor Scarlett O'Hara
Project Art Editor Lauren Adams
Design Assistants Ellie Bilbow, Elena Jarmoskaite
Pre-Production Producer Siu Chan
Senior Producer Louise Daly
Managing Editor Simon Hugo
Design Manager Guy Harvey
Art Director Lisa Lanzarini
Publisher Julie Ferris
Publishing Director Simon Beecroft

Written by Hannah Dolan
Inspirational models built by Tim Johnson
Photography by Gary Ombler

Dorling Kindersley would like to thank Randi Sørensen,
Henk van der Does, Fenella Blaize Charity, António Ricardo Silva,
Karen Mølgaard, Paul Hansford, and Robert Ekblom at the LEGO Group.
Thanks also to Beth Davies and Matt Jones at DK for editorial assistance.

First published in the United States in 2015
by DK Publishing, 345 Hudson Street,
New York, New York 10014
A Penguin Random House Company

18 19 10 9 8 7 6 5 4 3 2
010–195534–Aug/15

DK books are available at special discounts when purchased in
bulk for sales promotions, premiums, fund-raising, or educational
use. For details, contact: DK Publishing Special Markets,
345 Hudson Street, New York, New York 10014
SpecialSales@dk.com

A CIP catalog record for this book is available
from the Library of Congress.

ISBN: 978-1-4654-3589-7

Color reproduction by Transistics Data Technologies Pvt. Ltd.
Printed in China

www.LEGO.com
www.dk.com

A WORLD OF IDEAS:
SEE ALL THERE IS TO KNOW

Where will we go on our next adventure?